Renato Somberg Pfeffer
Lara F. C. Fonseca
Gabriella Grossi Daher

Challenges of the contemporary democratic state

Renato Somberg Pfeffer
Lara F. C. Fonseca
Gabriella Grossi Daher

Challenges of the contemporary democratic state

Intercultural relations and the question of fundamentalism-integrism

ScienciaScripts

Imprint
Any brand names and product names mentioned in this book are subject to trademark, brand or patent protection and are trademarks or registered trademarks of their respective holders. The use of brand names, product names, common names, trade names, product descriptions etc. even without a particular marking in this work is in no way to be construed to mean that such names may be regarded as unrestricted in respect of trademark and brand protection legislation and could thus be used by anyone.

Cover image: www.ingimage.com

This book is a translation from the original published under ISBN 978-620-2-04278-9.

Publisher:
Sciencia Scripts
is a trademark of
Dodo Books Indian Ocean Ltd. and OmniScriptum S.R.L publishing group

120 High Road, East Finchley, London, N2 9ED, United Kingdom
Str. Armeneasca 28/1, office 1, Chisinau MD-2012, Republic of Moldova, Europe
Managing Directors: Ieva Konstantinova, Victoria Ursu
info@omniscriptum.com

Printed at: see last page
ISBN: 978-620-8-52322-0

"Challenges of the contemporary democratic state: intercultural relations intercultural relations and the question of fundamentalism-integrism"

Author: Renato Somberg Pfeffer - coordinator of the scientific initiation research project at Fumec University

Scholarship students participating in the research project:

1. Lara Ferreira da Cunha Fonseca - scientific initiation scholarship holder from Fumec University
2. Gabriella Grossi Daher - Fumec University scientific initiation scholarship holder

Research project line: Democratic State: public administration, fundamental rights and guarantees. Period of implementation: 2009-2010

Funding organizations: Universidade Fumec (Fundagao Mineira de Educagao e Culture) and Fapemig (Minas Gerais Research Foundation)

Summary:

The beginning of the 21st century has seen the rise of religious fundamentalism all over the planet. This fundamentalist wave has stood out on the international stage as a promoter of various conflicts and its most frightening face is catastrophic mass transnational terrorism. Property and people are destroyed and killed indiscriminately in all parts of the world, in an unacceptable disregard for human rights, in the name of revenge legitimized by fanaticism. The reaction to terrorism, in turn, has also acquired the irrational character of a new crusade that puts the world economy and civil rights at risk. The aims of this research were to question the role of the democratic state in the face of this challenge, to critique the reaction of democratic states to religious fundamentalism and extremism, to analyze how fundamental rights and guarantees have been affected in this process, to debate the possibilities of intercultural dialogue in a world marked by cultural pluralism and to discuss the proposal of intercultural philosophy for the construction of a planetary ethic.

Summary

1. Introductory questions

1.1- Line of research to which the project is linked: Democratic State: public administration, fundamental rights and guarantees.

This research project was carried out with the support of Fumec University in 2009/10. The research was motivated by the unprecedented growth of religious fundamentalism, which has lasted from the end of the 20th century to the present day. This wave of fundamentalism has stood out on the international stage as a promoter of various conflicts and its most frightening aspect is the catastrophic transnational mass terrorism which, at the time the research was carried out, had the terrorist group Al Qaeda as its symbol. Property and people are destroyed and killed indiscriminately in all parts of the world, in an unacceptable disregard for human rights, in the name of revenge legitimized by fanaticism. The reaction to terrorism, in turn, has also acquired the irrational character of a new crusade that puts the world economy and civil rights at risk. The aims of this research were to question the role of the democratic state in the face of this challenge, to critique the reaction of democratic states to religious fundamentalism and intolerance, to analyze how fundamental rights and guarantees have been affected in this process, to debate the possibilities of intercultural dialogue in a world marked by cultural pluralism and to discuss the proposal of intercultural philosophy for building a planetary ethic.

1.2- Objectives

The new phase of world politics has generated a profusion of visions about the future: they predict the end of history, they foresee the return of rivalries between nation-states or even talk about the decline of the nation-state as a result of the conflict between tribalism and globalization. One of the most interesting visions of the future is that of political scientist Samuel Huntington. He argues that humanity is on a collision course between civilizations: "In this new world, local politics is the politics of ethnicity and world politics is the politics of civilizations. The rivalry of superpowers is replaced by the clash of civilizations" (1997, p. 21). Huntington states that the great divisions of humanity and the predominant source of conflict will be cultural. Despite the continuity of nation-states as the central subjects of global events, the main conflicts will be between groups from different civilizations.

The central focus of the conflicts of the 21st century will be between Western civilization and non-Western civilization, and between Western civilization and non-Western civilization. Firstly, because they have different conceptions of the relationship between God and man, between citizens and the state, between parents and children, between freedom and authority, between equality and hierarchy. Secondly, the world is getting smaller and the awareness of the difference between civilizations is growing. Thirdly, and above all, the religious fundamentalism and fundamentalism present in all religions are major factors at the beginning of the 21st century. This research focuses on precisely this last issue: religious fundamentalism and its most harmful aspect, terrorism. Fundamentalism offers its followers absolute certainties and unquestionable guidelines, allowing them to live in security. These currents renounce hermeneutics as a mediation between sacred texts and the cultural contexts in which they are read. God would have revealed these texts, so they would be immutable and should be understood literally. The result of this is a denial of the historical-critical method and a belief in the literal applicability of these texts to the concrete situations of life.

The development of religious fundamentalism is linked to the transformations that have taken place in modernity. Faced with pluralism and the constant changes brought about by capitalist expansion, traditionalist religious segments react by returning to the deepest foundations of their religion. Traditionalism, dogmatism and religious intolerance are intended to be responses to the relativization of revealed truth, the breakdown of authority and autonomy for the formation of new religious identities.

Traditions are not, in themselves, but. Through them we build our identities. *"But fundamentalism falls into a misuse of tradition, which prevents recreation, a natural requirement of our historical condition"* (RIESGO, Inddito, p. 42). In other words, tradition cannot prevent the changes that are sometimes necessary, it must serve as a mediator so that we can reposition ourselves to face the challenges of the present. Fundamentalists' a-historical affirmations of traditions hinder progress and violate the cognitive capacity of human beings, undermining their possibilities. The proclamation of definitive answers to the ultimate questions of humanity places fundamentalism in clear contradiction with the pluralism of answers promoted by the infinity of religions on the planet. Reified dogmatism makes dialogue impossible and the most damaging effect of this is intolerance and the authoritarian attempt to impose the beliefs of one religion on another. However, it is important to emphasize that the fundamentalist phenomenon constitutes a *"marginal zone", "the dark face of the various religions"* (KIENZLER, 2000, p. 11).

Fundamentalism, as the dark side of religiosity, still has a more dangerous social aspect: fundamentalism. This uses violent methods to defend its political and ideological positions. Its ultimate goal is the seizure of political power with the aim of establishing religious totalitarian states. Fundamentalism criticizes Western society, accusing it of imperialist policies from both a cultural and economic point of view. While fundamentalism is born out of a search for a purer and more authentic spirituality, fundamentalism originates in the resentment of those excluded from Western society. Both movements began to grow towards the end of the 1970s, presenting themselves as an alternative to the prevailing ideological bipolarization. Progress was seen by these currents as the path to destruction and salvation would only be possible through religion itself, which was considered the only true religion.

Religious pluralism, contrary to what fundamentalist-integrism advocates, is legitimate and necessary given the infinite distance between creator and creature. Forgetting the insufficiency of religious languages to cover this distance leads us to the ethnocentric and racist attitudes typical of fundamentalism. The most plausible vision for understanding man's relationship with God would be to admit that all peoples are chosen and that God manifests himself in different ways for each one. This vision legitimizes pluralism and promotes a harmonious relationship between peoples.

This doesn't seem to be the dominant tone of the late 20th and early 21st centuries, where fundamentalist tendencies are growing in all the world's major religions. These religious fundamentalisms have stood out on the international stage as the promoters of various conflicts. Property and people are destroyed and killed indiscriminately in all parts of the world, in an unacceptable disregard for human rights, in the name of revenge legitimized by religious fanaticism. The reaction to terrorism, in turn, 1amЬёш has acquired the irrational character of a new crusade that puts the world economy and civil rights at risk.

What should the role of the democratic state be in the face of this challenge? How are the various states reacting? Is there an alternative to fundamentalism and its most harmful aspect, fundamentalism?

1.3- Justification

The new international scenario is characterized by the growing internationalization, integration and complexity of our societies. This results in a series of uncertainties regarding the paths to follow. We live in a time of anomie. This concept, Durkheimian in its origin (DURKHEIM, 2000, p. 311), was used to characterize the moral crisis that European industrial society was going through in the 19th century. The transition from mechanical solidarity (based on tradition and/or affectivity) to organic solidarity (based on rationality) occurred so quickly that the foundations of the social order were lost. The founder of sociology believed that the new mode of production would be able to solve this problem gradually, since the resulting division of labor would help men to become interdependent. Only then would order be restored. Marx (1986), taking the opposite route, defended the thesis that the division of labor would generate alienation.

Both analyses certainly don't apply precisely to the new industrial revolution of the second half of the 20th century and the consequent process of internationalization. However, the phenomenon of anomie typical of times of accelerated change remains and is exacerbated today as the new human condition is marked by multiculturalism. This is not a new fact in human history, on the contrary, it is a historical constant. What is new is the awareness of the importance of this phenomenon. This forces us to question the development of a social dynamic marked by intercultural relations. A new ethic of coexistence between these different cultures has to be built. An ethic that renounces the logic of imposition in order to guarantee the survival of different cultural worlds. The question is how to guarantee individual rights combined with an authentic dialogue between cultures.

The Enlightenment dream of an emancipated society was based on a triple rationality: the free market economy, contractualist theory through democratic participation and a moral life based on practical reason and utilitarianism. This dream ended up failing largely due to the hegemony of instrumental reason, which was put at the service of logic and capital. Progress came to be identified solely with productivity. In the 20th century, the welfare state gave the illustrated project a new lease of life by correcting some of its distortions. The rearticulation of the liberal project, combined with the failure of real socialism, led to the phenomenon of economic globalization. The boundaries of market and production, capital and technology are becoming less and less important. The free market is quite effective in its task of ordering the economy, but on the other hand, it causes distortions by promoting the accumulation of surplus value in the hands of a minority of owners. This concentration of economic power is the great enemy of democracy. How can democracy in the economy be reconciled with market rationality? How can the democratic state guarantee the fundamental rights of the individual in a liberal economy?

So far, it is well known that economic hegemony, without political control, has not been able to avoid the chaos of monetary turbulence. Much less has it been able to prevent the worsening of social inequalities internationally or within national states. Global competitiveness has coexisted with global social disintegration. This whole process is aggravated by the fundamentalist-integrist wave sweeping the contemporary world. The effect of this process of rupture between functionality and the meaning of life, between the market and the community, between the role of the state and the rights of the individual, is an identity crisis that is perhaps the great social pathology of modernity. Paradoxically, the globalized world has produced a reaction that is embodied in the search for difference, for identity. This is the rebirth of the community and local movement, which seeks identity in opposition to the global movement. While these movements have the beneficial effect of guaranteeing the survival of particular identities, they can also generate intercultural hatred.

Intercultural dialogue can serve to find points of encounter that allow us to perceive equality in difference, paving the way for harmonious and fruitful coexistence. This seems to be the only way to overcome the extremes of a dehumanized, unjust society with fundamentalist tendencies. An intercultural philosophy must be understood as the possibility of dialogue and interaction between cultures, challenging the purely economic perspective of globalization. Interculturality seeks dialogue that denies any notion of superiority and therefore does not accept the absolute certainties of fundamentalism. Through it, we can discover intuitions and convictions shared by a large part of humanity, and the democratic state has a fundamental role to play in this process.

The critical nature of this dialogue can help confirm the universality of human rights, which serve as a standard and limit for other rights. Cultural differences that go against these rights and the common good should not be allowed. On the other hand, differences that enrich the cultural heritage as a humanizing medium should be encouraged. Human rights should therefore serve as a criterion for deciding what is acceptable or not in a given culture. In this context, the human invariants found in different cultures must be transformed into transcultural ones, guaranteeing the possibility of dialogue. A dialogue that starts from the recognition of the particular, but seeks universalization. Otherwise, if we can't find something in common in the other that will be the foundation of a planetary ethics, there will be no solution but to accept exclusionary political models.

2. Theoretical aspects of terrorism

2.1 War, terrorism and man inhabited by the pulse of death

The 8th century was a landmark of tragedy and progress for Western civilization. The two world wars and the totalitarian regimes killed millions of people. On the other hand, mankind reached unimaginable levels of cultural, scientific and technological development.

The monstrosities perpetrated by human beings are not exclusive to the past century. Already in the Bible there are various accounts of crimes committed by the most diverse characters. There, crimes were transformed into sins. In fact, barbarism permeates the whole of human history, producing fear and horror. Paradoxically, the counterpoint to these tragedies is an entire critical, legal, artistic and technological development.

Freud even put forward the hypothesis that human progress has concluded a pact with barbarism in the preface to his book "Moses and Monotheism" (1939). The philosopher Walter Benjamin (1985) believes that the traditional dichotomy between civilization and barbarism is a farce. For Benjamin (1985: 225) "there has never been a monument of culture that was not also a monument of barbarism. And just as culture is not free of barbarism, neither is the process of transmitting culture".

The terrorist attacks of September 11 and the continuing technological advances of the new millennium give the impression that the 20th century is not yet over. Are war and progress really inseparable? Are culture and barbarism part of the same process? Terrorist attacks, in particular, raise another question: what makes someone turn into a human bomb and why?

Freud wrote a text entitled "Current considerations on war and death" (1915) a few months after the start of the First World War. In it, Freud wondered whether humanity wasn't heading inevitably towards destruction.

After all, said the author, it would be natural to assume that human beings, constituted in crime and by crime, would put an end to their existence through crime.

In another article, Freud asks himself "Why war?" (1933). His answer comes from a basic finding of psychoanalysis:

> There are only two types of human pulse: those that tend to preserve and those that tend to destroy (...). Neither is less essential than the other: the phenomena of life arise from the confluent or mutually contrary action of both (...). The difficulty of isolating the two kinds of pulse in their real manifestations is, in fact, what has hitherto prevented us from recognizing them (FREUD, 1933, p. 209-210).

Freud clearly distinguishes between the human drive to destroy and the drive to preserve life. All two are of total importance to man, and our challenge remains to isolate these two types of drive. The crime, barbarism and genocide generated by humanity are typical of a man inhabited by the death drive.

The reflections contained in this article aim to point out some ways of interpreting one of the most terrible manifestations of contemporary human barbarism: fundamentalist terrorism. This kind of terrorism has led to the trivialization of the value of life, in flagrant disrespect for others and human rights. Furthermore, the name of God has been appropriated by terrorists and by the very states that fight it.

Fundamentalist terrorism is not exclusive to Islam. Fundamentalists are found in Islam, Judaism and Christianity. The confusion between Islam and terrorism is a mistake, "it amounts to forgetting the essence of the radical Abrahamic monotheism present in Judaism, Islam and Christianity" (PROCOPIO, 2001, p. 71). Leaving aside the stereotype that equates Islamism with terrorism, this article aims to raise some questions about terrorism today, about the conceptual issue that these acts involve and about the reaction of states to this phenomenon.

2.2- Terrorism in history and today

International terrorism is a recurring problem in human history. It has been present since the existence of the great constitutional states in world history. As Procopio explains, "the terrorism of persecution, injustice and intolerance has never been a minor problem for human society" (PROCOPIO, 2001, p. 62). Paradoxically, almost all states, with very few exceptions, have always considered it a marginal pathology.

Its most expressive form arose with the growth of capitalism, but regardless of the degree of intensity, terrorism in itself is a way of expressing a certain dissatisfaction with the ruling power. Terror has been practiced since Biblical times. At the dawn of the Christian era they are evident. "Terrorist acts, or actions considered as such, filled the entire period in which the great constitutional states were constituted and capitalist modernity was affirmed". (SUGAHARA, 2008, p. 1). Sugahara also states that these strategies of terror gained strength with the world wars of the 20th century in the form of national liberation struggles.

In fact, we can say that there have been two major and distinct moments of international terrorism in the contemporary world. The first was during the Cold War, when all the tensions in the diplomatic and military fields, as well as terrorist attacks, were linked to it. Terrorist attacks were generally located in the wars of independence of former colonies. This geographical restriction meant that there were no significant waves of international instability. The second period, which saw a marked change in violence indicators, was post-Cold War terrorism in the 1990s. This period saw the emergence of a complex network of agents who escaped the control of states and were endowed with a complex variety of technological and biotechnological resources. A highlight of this new type of terrorism is the individual's willingness to commit suicide.

A classic example of a terrorist network that experienced these two historical moments was Al Qaeda, responsible for the terrorist attacks of September 11, 2001. This network underwent structural changes over time, redirecting the focus of its efforts in the 1990s from fighting Soviet communists to fighting the influence of global capitalism represented by the United States of America.

This shift in the focus of terrorist attacks is related to capitalist globalization, which shows a shift in power from the national to the global sphere. At the same time, and in the opposite direction, the struggle to maintain local identities has given rise to nationalist movements based on the valorization of regional culture and the strength of tradition. According to Sdrgio Paulo Rouanet (2005), modern society is crossed by paradoxes, contradictory and at the same time complementary forces. An example of this are the lakes of identity within groups, which strengthen and legitimize them, encourage exacerbated nationalism, xenophobia, rivalries and wars between nations, and even international terrorism of a fundamentalist nature. Terrorism, as part of this process, is generally associated with radical left-wing groups, but many right-wing governments also use it to eliminate political opponents.

Along the same lines, Marilena Chaul (2002) also associates post-modern barbarism - one of the manifestations of which is fundamentalist terrorism - with capitalist globalization. According to Chaul, the current capitalist model is marked by a strong transformation in the relationship between space and time that causes two opposite and simultaneous phenomena. On the one hand, space and time are fragmented and, on the other, they are compressed into the here and now, under the effects of the new information technologies.

In fact, the fragmentation and dispersion of space and time condition their reunification under an undifferentiated space and an ephemeral time, or under a space that is reduced to a flat surface of images and under a time that has lost its depth and is reduced to the movement of fast and fleeting images (CHAUI, 2002, p. 127).

Post-modernity has created a market whose rationality is marked by the ephemeral, the disposable and which reduces the citizen to the figure of a consumer, and the worker is as disposable as the product he manufactures/sells. This process has led to a weakening of the state, and a kind of privatization of the polis and the res publica is evident. "The first effect of this privatization is depoliticization. The privatization of public space and depoliticization are alarming signs that we may be facing the risk of the end of politics." (CHAUI, 2002, p. 131). Today's depoliticization is extremely conducive to the emergence of charismatic and fanatical religious leaders.

The profound transformations that capitalist society is undergoing mean that man feels at the mercy of the whims of fortune; of chance and luck. Individuals lack control over the circumstances of their own lives. "Since they do not have control over the circumstances of their lives and are driven by the desire for goods that do not seem to depend on them, humans are naturally inhabited by two passions, fear and hope." (CHAUI, 2002, p. 136). These circumstances, combined with depoliticization, tend to encourage religiosity and, more specifically, fundamentalism.

Chaui says that the return of religious fundamentalism, which would be one of the manifestations of barbarism, puts society at risk. She also points out the dangerous post-modern tendency to assume that religion can be held responsible for social order and cohesion. The speeches of Sharon, Bin Laden and Bush, according to the author, are clear expressions of the impossibility of politics under the fundamentalism of revealed monotheistic religions. "With them, politics gives way to violence as a purification against evil, and politicians give way to prophets, that is, interpreters of the divine will, infallible leaders." (CHAUI, 2002, p. 136). The reflection of all this is the terrorist acts practiced by religious leaders or heads of state.

2.3- The different faces of violence and terrorism

It is interesting to note that, despite various definitions proposed by different theorists, there is still no universally accepted definition of what terrorism is. This lack of support leads to a series of problems and controversies in people's imaginations, for example, when it comes to differentiating between terror and terrorism. However, it is clear that there is a cause and effect relationship here. Terror is a psychological or moral effect caused by terrorism and, in turn, specifically affects the victims of terrorist attacks.

Despite the lack of a univocal definition, the characterization of a terrorist act can be related to a few key factors. Firstly, it is absolutely certain that there is no such thing as a terrorist act without a political purpose. Secondly, they use violence, whether physical or psychological, to benefit groups that are dissatisfied with the current political model. Thirdly, terrorism aims to trigger in people who are unhappy with the system the perception that, even in such an asymmetrical condition of power, their discontent can be changeable. Finally, this perception that it is possible to change the social structure aims to generate reactions in disgruntled groups that alter the power relations in favor of the group that carried out the terrorist act. From this general characterization, it can be inferred that a terrorist act has its own rationale. As Pape (2003, p. 4) states, "even when suicide attackers are irrational or fanatical, the group leaders who recruit and direct them are not".

Using the work of Michael Foucault as a theoretical reference, Saly Wellausen argues that terrorism "is the counterpoint to dominant power, as a threatening and diffuse presence, acting by surprise, spreading fear and destruction wherever it goes" (WELLAUSEN, 2002, p. 83). The author points to the growing phenomenon of social fragmentation and the emergence of isolated groups at the end of the 20th century, a clear trend in a world marked by globalization, as an essential factor in the increase in terrorist attacks.

Allied to the issue of social fragmentation, at the beginning of this millennium we are experiencing a disconnection between the needs of society and government policies. This lack of harmony between state and society increases the tendency for violent conflicts to arise. Terrorist acts are a case in point.

Throughout history, acts of violence have not gone unnoticed and have been widely recorded. Five forms of violence stand out, differing in their organizational structure, the public they reach or the goal they aim to achieve. Three of them are a kind of method or process, and the other two are the forms themselves.

In terms of process, the most traditional model of violence is war. It is institutionalized, ritualized and paradoxically seeks peace. The cruelty of war, however great, admits rules and laws, recognizes the enemy as a person, respects prisoners, spares civilians and presupposes the possibility of a return to a time of peace. Other methods are massacre and genocide. Massacre is marked by the savage unleashing of hatred, giving vent to the most terrible destructive impulses: prisoners are killed, children and old people are executed, torture becomes trivial. Genocide reaches the pinnacle of horror through the total elimination of individuals.

But it is through the form, i.e. extermination and terrorism, that violence actually manifests itself. According to Wellausen (2002), the two are antagonistic, with the first aiming for quantitative violence, mass destruction, using massacres and genocides. Examples of extermination throughout history include Stalinism, Nazism and the dropping of atomic bombs on the Japanese cities of Hiroshima and Nagasaki. It's important to point out that in all three cases these are forms of state violence, each in its own way, but always using methods of torture and massacre that are prejudiced and unjust in their essence.

Terrorism, on the other hand, has a more clearly defined focus of destruction, aims for qualitative violence and uses almost surgical methods to achieve this.

For Norberto Bobbio, terrorism, as a common recourse to violence, distinguishes different situations, depending on its political weight. It can either be an instrument of government to maintain itself in power, or an instrument of national liberation in dominated nations; in one way or another, terrorism is always the breaking of the order imposed by the dominant power. (...) Terrorism as a one-off practice is an expression of the need for political affirmation (WELLAUSEN, 2002, p. 89).

The power relations inscribed in the terrorist act can be analyzed using two fundamental concepts from Foucault's work: the microphysics of power and games of truth. The idea of the microphysics of power emphasizes that power is not found in a purely institutionalized dimension; there are levels of power that cross the entire social body. Power is found and exercised in hierarchies, in various forms of control, in surveillance and in prohibitions. People constantly watch and try to control each other.

The idea of truth games explains how power and knowledge are articulated within discourses, in other words, in the tactical elements of a field of power relations. Power produces knowledge and truth, and power and knowledge are not separate, since knowledge as an effect remains within power, articulating itself within discourse. In other words, Foucault addresses the conception of what is considered true in a given time and space. Power and knowledge are neither eternal nor immutable; they are in the spatiality of pure actuality.

The strategy of the terrorist minorities is based on the microphysics of power when it goes through two stages: one within the terrorist group itself, and the other when the attack is directed outwards and unfolds in waves of violence throughout society. If we look closely, the presence of Foucauldian concepts is evident not only in the terrorist group, but also in the society affected, which, through individual and collective surveillance, determines a certain type of behaviour and socialization. Terrorism is the strategy of an omnipresent and diffuse power that acts by sampling. In other words, it doesn't need to destroy the whole of society in order to achieve its goal, because it's enough to target a part of the enemy in order to establish fear and panic.

In short, all the terror, violence and barbarity of terrorist acts stem from a dissatisfaction with the power in force, a way of expressing this opposition to the greater power within society itself. In order to achieve their objectives of establishing fear and panic in society, terrorist attacks need to guarantee their visibility and enunciability. Visibility is the action of the terrorist group's punctual choice in a given social space, causing the fact to have repercussions in society. Enunciability is the declaration of the perpetrator of the crime.

This brings us to the relationship between terrorist strategies and the media. By exercising its legitimate role as a disseminator of information, the media has become terrorism's greatest ally. Television appears here as the main means of communication in this universe, which, through teleterrorism, acts as a sounding board. It broadcasts terrorist acts in real time, often as a spectacle. The media, when sensationalist, does much of the work for the terrorists. In the name of audiences, it creates a general panic, becoming a disseminator of the messages that terrorist groups want to spread.

In this context of massification and the definition of social attitudes, what Foucault worked on in the categories of power becomes compatible. Power, in the case of terrorism, cuts across all existing social relations, ensuring the spread of violence within the entire social body. "Terrorism has become 'an eye that sees' all of society through the punctual action of its strategies, as a new form of panoptism that makes humanity transparent and vulnerable." (WELLAUSEN, 2002, p. 98).

Another interesting attempt to define and analyze terrorist attacks is in Mijolla-Mello's book "The Pleasure of Thought" (1992). Aiming to explain the origins of disorder and barbarism, the author analyzes the problem of libertinism in the works of Marques de Sade. She raises the hypothesis that the gratuitousness of crime, its lack of motive, is related to the notion of apathy. Sade, as is well known, dealt with violence within a philosophy in which the pursuit of personal pleasure involves the annihilation of the other.

Based on this assumption, we can consider that the real foundation of all barbarities lies precisely in the disidentification from the other. It is "a disidentification with the victim in the name of an identification with a higher principle" (MIJOLLA-MELLO, 2005, p. 174) which then allows cruelty to emerge.

In identifying the origin of barbarism and disorder in the process of disidentifying from the other, Mijolla-Mello points out the need to differentiate between terrorism and insurrection, although he notes that both foment disorder, use violence and depend on a manifestation of force.

Terrorism, specifically, aims to install terror, to destabilize order without a greater objective, with a target apparently chosen at random. It is violence in response to violence, a form of disorder to explode an order that is itself founded on terror. Terrorism refuses to recognize the existence of the other. Insurrection, on the other hand, tries to bring about change, it has a defined target and aims to establish a new order.

Within this same scope, a distinction can be made between two concepts that are often confused in the popular imagination: anarchism and terrorism. Both may appear to have the same cause, but they are essentially different. While terrorism uses extermination, terror and coercion in the form of extreme violence, anarchism defends individual freedom through self-management, given that this characteristic is often impeded in traditional power relations. It is a libertarian political action with well-defined ideals.

Regardless of whether we are talking about terrorism, insurrections or anarchism, the reaction of the state to these movements has most often taken the form of "defensive terrorism". This attempt to re-establish order at any cost ends up involving humanity in a paradox, because the violence with which the states have reacted has provoked more and more protests and revolts.

2.4- States' reaction to terrorism

The absence of a clear and universal definition of the concept of terrorism sets a dangerous precedent for the state to use institutional violence to combat it. In particular, the government of the United States of America has been questioned about its attitudes on this issue. The economic and political prominence of this nation in the second half of the 20th century consolidated, both in American society and in its leaders, the idea of a supposed and desired hegemony. Taking advantage of the global crisis in the capitalist world after the Second World War, this supremacy was imposed by the superpower on its area of influence through institutions like NATO and economic recovery plans like the Marshall Plan, among others. Today, international terrorism mainly threatens this hegemony.

Terrorist threats have forced the United States to take extreme measures to defend itself.

By proclaiming themselves guardians of peace and seeking to combat terrorist attacks, the Americans have introduced into their ideology an abstraction of their own power, based on the assumption that they possess the highest moral values that should be brought to other cultures. Madeleine Albright, former US ambassador to the UN, once said: "we fly higher, we see from above, and we know what's best for the world" (ALBRIGHT, apud SUGAHARA, 2008, p. 5). This speech shows the superpower's self-esteem.

The violent and hateful reaction to terrorism has turned the whole fight against these abominable movements into another "holy war", especially after the attacks of September 11, 2001. Sughara (2008) thoroughly analyzes the role of the United States as the supposed guardian of world peace after this episode. Drawing on the reflections of three of the most important sociologists of the 20th century (Poland's Zygmunt Bauman, Germany's Ulrich Beck and Britain's Anthony Giddens), he shows that the type of action taken by the US government after these attacks is recurrent throughout its history. Classic examples of this attitude are the atomic bombs dropped on the Japanese cities of Hiroshima and Nagasaki and the authorization to use surgical strikes against targets in Afghanistan under the Clinton administration, when the US embassies in Kenya and Tanzania were attacked by terrorists.

Afghanistan itself, the victim of a US operation under the Bush administration after the September 11 attack, would be another example of this US policy. In relation to this attack specifically, it is important to note that the fear and terror generated by the fall of the twin towers helped to build a broad sense of solidarity around the US. President Bush was able, in the initial phase of the conflict, to use this international solidarity to justify unilateral US action against terror. Rarely in history has a government been able to build such a broad consensus to occupy another sovereign nation.

Based on this assessment, Sughara (2008) defends three hypotheses for the development of his research on terrorism and insecurity in the post-9/11 world: 1) Terrorism is the new substitute for the geo-rich threat, which during the Cold War was interpreted as the communist threat; 2) The fear resulting from the violent attacks of September 11 helped to construct the false premise that the freedom of individuals should be restricted in the name of collective security; 3) The culture of American exceptionalism, to which part of the responsibility for the messianic policy of the war on terror is attributed, is not exclusive to the Bush administration or the Republican party.

ТашЬёш Procopio (2001) compares the United States' reaction to the recent attacks with ancient historical events:

It's worth remembering the Platt Amendment of 1901, which empowered the United States to invade Cuba. This amendment, impregnated with the concepts of the Monroe Doctrine, paved the way for the appearance, in 1904, of the Roosevelt corollary, accompanied by the hated 'big club'. In substance, it was almost identical to the model of the club now displayed by Texan George W. Bush in his savage crusade against terrorism (PROCOPIO, 2001, p. 68).

A century later, the Big Stick has reappeared in a much more modern version. The current US reaction to terrorism brings with it the power of nuclear weapons, but these are useless in terms of internal security. Procopio also points out that "unfortunately, there are relatively few voices calling for the use of military force in the fight against terror" (PROCOPIO, 2001, p. 68). In fact, the use of violence to combat terrorism is totally questionable, because, to date, violence has not been able to eliminate the barbarism it represents. Violence can only bring more violence and "the peace of the cemeteries is not the peace that is desired in international relations" (PROCOPIO, 2001, p. 68).

If we take a general overview of the world after the September 11 attacks, we can see that the moral condemnation embedded in the term terrorist has grown along with the wave of the fight against terrorism. A duality between good and evil is becoming apparent, as is the collision between civilization and the so-called barbarians. It is this situation that opens up space for state intervention as the supposed maintainer of social order. States then begin to intervene arbitrarily in the lives of individuals and, consequently, in the freedom of their citizens, always in the name of maintaining collective and individual security. By creating and maintaining a state of tension, terrorist actions justify defensive state terrorism.

Nowadays there is a kind of pseudo-situation of terror that distances society from the real sources of tension and anxiety in the contemporary world. This situation needs to be reviewed, otherwise the idea that security and freedom are incompatible will spread ever more rapidly.

Sugahara (2008, p. 90) argues that the idea of security in the post-9/11 world is a myth and that the role played by the United States of America needs to be reassessed. This nation, with its prominent role in international relations, has little interest in dialoguing with others and has become the main force behind the creation/maintenance of state terrorism. Americans, in general, are even willing to give up their civil liberties so that the government can act freely in the fight against terrorism. This nullification of the capacity for self-reflection generated by fear is a dangerous precedent that greatly increases the power of security experts.

The collapse of conventional morality and the principles of human security in the anti-terror war make it clear that the greatest shortcoming of US policy in international relations is its disregard for inequalities. This shortcoming highlights the fact that the world, especially the United States of America, continues to try to respond to terrorism with practices that have never worked in the past.

All attempts by the United States to decimate terrorism through military violence have failed. On the contrary, "the violence and waste taught in movies and other channels of dominant culture strengthen the networks that sustain terror" (PROCOPIO, 2001, p. 64). The terrorist movement has several ways of escaping or even sustaining itself. Coercing it with a single act of war is a sure path to failure.

The problem is that security experts are generally not experts in human rights, Arab culture, religion, sociology or anthropology - among all the other specialties needed to have a view of the whole and not a partial view of the big picture. (SUGAHARA, 2008, p. 91).

2.5- Terrorism as a sin to be fought

Western Christian civilization, in particular, needs to admit its share of the blame for acts of terror. This civilization has not applied its principles of morality and ethics and has accepted living with injustice. A society that accepts injustice and corruption reduces the space for the full exercise of citizenship and makes man less and less the subject of his history.

Any kind of fanaticism ignores the freedom to challenge and has a worldview that is entirely focused on the absolute truth of its belief. Terrorism represents a global contestation of modernity, insofar as it has become too complex and difficult to accept.

Terrorist fundamentalism represents, in a retrograde way, the shapelessness of this globalized world in which we live.

Terrorism is a typical scourge of a civilization that has turned man into a commodity. It is a plague that democratic states have no control over. Militarizing against terrorist acts is a necessity for those who believe in the recognition of otherness and work for democracy. On the other hand, defensive state terrorism has targeted innocents and left aside the liberal and ethical principles that humanity should aim for. Fighting terrorism without abandoning ethical principles is the difficult mission of the forces fighting for civilization.

In the Bible, crimes have been transformed into sins and the divine commandments, as well as the prophets' cries of protest and love, act to limit barbarism. It is interesting to note that the Torah does not forbid war; on the contrary, it imposes the duty of self-defense and fighting for our rights (Deut. 21:10). If on the one hand it is sad to resort to war, on the other hand there are times when it is necessary to do so and the legislator feels the need to impose limits on it. In war, human feelings are stifled and the law of Moses imposes prescriptions so that the conscience of goodness is not lost.

Far from being an exclusively Jewish legacy, these prescriptions have been present in various human cultures that have been able to develop a critical, legal and artistic counterpoint to terror. Paradoxically, monstrosities can stimulate the creative capacity of human beings to combat them and put us on the road to peace. If the maxim of some biblical exegetes that crime, war and monstrosities are the manifestation of man's evil instinct *(yetzer hard)* is correct, we can also assume that mankind's good instinct *(yetzer hatov)* can also lead us to the fulfillment of the prophecy that there will be a time when "people will not rise against people with the sword and they will no longer teach war" (Micah 4:3).

3. Interreligious dialogue and the construction of citizenship in a globalized world as an alternative to fundamentalism-integrism: the contribution of Brazilian religious syncretism.

3.1- The uncertainties generated by intercultural relations in a globalized world

The Enlightenment dream of an emancipated society was based on a triple rationality: the free market economy, contractualist theory through democratic participation and a moral life based on practical reason and utilitarianism. This dream ended up failing largely due to the hegemony of instrumental reason, which was put at the service of logic and capital. Progress came to be identified solely as productivity. In the 20th century, the welfare state gave the illustrated project a new lease of life by correcting some of its distortions. The rearticulation of the liberal project, combined with the failure of real socialism, led to the phenomenon of economic globalization. The boundaries of market and production, capital and technology are becoming less and less important. The free market is quite effective in its task of ordering the economy, but on the other hand, it causes distortions by promoting the accumulation of surplus value in the hands of a minority of owners. This concentration of economic power is the great enemy of democracy.

Economic hegemony, without political control, has not been able to avoid the chaos of monetary turbulence. Much less has it been able to prevent the worsening of social inequalities internationally or within nation states. The effect of this process of rupture between functionality and the meaning of life, between the market and the community, between the role of the state and the rights of the individual, is an identity crisis that is perhaps the great social pathology of modernity. Paradoxically, the globalized world has produced a reaction that is embodied in the search for difference, for identity. This is the rebirth of the community and local movement, which seeks identity in opposition to the global movement. While on the one hand these movements have the beneficial effect of guaranteeing the survival of particular identities, on the other hand they can generate intercultural friction.

In this new international scenario, the growing internationalization, integration and complexity of our societies stand out. As a result, there are a number of uncertainties about the way forward. We live in an age of anomie. This concept was used by sociology

(DURKHEIM 2000, p. 311) to characterize the moral crisis that European industrial society was going through in the 19th century. The transition from mechanical solidarity, based on tradition, to organic solidarity, based on rationality, occurred so quickly that the foundations of social order were lost. The phenomenon of anomie is typical of societies undergoing rapid change and can be used as a paradigm for today's world. Anomie has even worsened in a reality where the human condition is marked by the multiculturalism generated by capitalist globalization.

The multicultural age is not a new fact in human history; in fact, it is a historical constant. What is new is the awareness of the importance of this phenomenon. This forces us to question the development of a social dynamic marked by intercultural relations. A new ethic of coexistence between these cultures has to be built. An ethic that renounces the logic of imposition in order to guarantee the survival of different cultural worlds. The question is how to guarantee individual rights in conjunction with a genuine dialogue between cultures.

3.2- Fighting fundamentalism: a defense of pluralism and dialogue

The new phase of world politics has generated a profusion of visions about the future: they predict the end of history, they foresee the return of rivalries between nation-states or even talk about the decline of the nation-state as a result of the conflict between tribalism and globalization. One of the most interesting visions of the future is that of political scientist Samuel Huntington. He argues that humanity is on a collision course between civilizations: "In this new world, local politics is the politics of ethnicity and world politics is the politics of civilizations. The rivalry of superpowers is replaced by the clash of civilizations" (HUNTINGTON 1997, p.21). Huntington states that the great divisions of humanity and the predominant source of conflict will be cultural. Despite the continuity of nation-states as the central subjects of global events, the main conflicts will be between different civilizations.

The central focus of the conflicts of the 21st century, according to Huntington, will be between Western civilization and non-Western civilization, and the latter among themselves. Firstly, because they have different conceptions of the relationship between God and man, between citizens and the state, between parents and children, between freedom and authority, between equality and hierarchy. Secondly, the world is getting smaller and the awareness of the difference between civilizations is growing. Thirdly, and above all, the religious fundamentalism present in all religions is a striking factor at the beginning of the 21st century.

The issue of religious fundamentalism is fundamental to a better understanding of the contemporary world. Fundamentalism offers its followers absolute certainties and unquestionable guidelines, allowing them to live in security. These currents renounce hermeneutics as a means of mediating between sacred texts. The result is a denial of the historical-critical method and a belief in the literal applicability of these texts to the concrete situations of life. The development of this religious fundamentalist wave is linked to the transformations that have taken place in modernity. Faced with pluralism and the constant changes brought about by the capitalist advance, traditionalist religious segments react by returning to the deepest foundations of their religion.

Traditions are not, in themselves, but. Through them we construct our identities. As Riesgo (2006, p. 42) states, fundamentalism falls into a misuse of tradition, which prevents re-creation, a master requirement of our historical condition. In other words, tradition cannot prevent the changes that are sometimes necessary, it must serve as a mediator so that we can get back on our feet in the face of the challenges of the present. Fundamentalists' a-historical affirmations of traditions hinder progress and violate the cognitive capacity of human beings, undermining their possibilities. The proclamation of definitive answers to humanity's ultimate questions puts fundamentalism in clear contradiction with the pluralism of answers promoted by the infinity of religions on the planet. However, it is important to emphasize that the fundamentalist phenomenon constitutes a "marginal zone" (KIENZLER 2000, p.11), the dark side of the various religions.

Religious pluralism, contrary to what fundamentalism advocates, is legitimate and necessary given the infinite distance between creator and creature. Forgetting the insufficiency of religious languages to cover this distance leads us to ethnocentric and racist attitudes, typical of fundamentalism. The most plausible vision for understanding man's relationship with God would be to admit that all peoples are chosen and that God manifests himself in different ways for each one. This vision legitimizes pluralism and promotes a harmonious relationship between peoples.

This doesn't seem to be the dominant tone of the late 20th and early 21st centuries, where fundamentalist tendencies are growing in all the world's major religions. These religious fundamentalisms have stood out on the international stage as promoters of various terrorist acts. The reaction to terrorism, in turn, has also acquired the irrational character of a new crusade that puts the world economy and civil rights at risk. One of the great questions facing humanity today is precisely this: is there an alternative to fundamentalism?

The only alternative to fundamentalism is intercultural dialogue. Only through it can we find equality in difference, opening up space for harmonious and fruitful coexistence. This seems to be the only way to overcome the extremes of a dehumanized, unjust society with fundamentalist tendencies. An intercultural philosophy must be understood as the possibility of dialogue and interaction between cultures, challenging the purely economic perspective of globalization. Interculturality seeks a dialogue that denies any notion of superiority and therefore does not accept the absolute certainties of fundamentalism. Through it, we can discover intuitions and convictions shared by a large part of humanity, and the democratic state has a fundamental role to play in this process.

The need for intercultural dialogue in a globalized world can help confirm the universality of human rights, which serve as the norm and limit for other rights. Cultural differences that go against these rights and the common good should not be allowed. On the other hand, differences that enrich the cultural heritage as a humanizing medium should be encouraged. Human rights should therefore serve as a yardstick for deciding what is acceptable or not in a given culture. In this context, the human invariants found in different cultures must be transformed into transcultural ones, guaranteeing the possibility of dialogue. Otherwise, there will be no solution but to accept exclusionary political models.

Human rights are above any specific cultural tradition, as if they were something transcendent to them; they are the heritage of all humanity because they are the memory of its struggle for freedom. Intercultural dialogue, in turn, would make it possible to bring together cultural traditions that have experienced histories of liberation. Cultures would thus exchange experiences, enriching each other.

By respecting cultural plurality, we would be moving towards a universal culture of human liberation. Universality would be guaranteed by the solidarity participation of all cultures in this project (FORNET-BETANCOURT 2001, p. 293). The transcendence mentioned above would enable an ethical critique of cultures based on the universality of human rights. According to Fornet-Betancourt, there is no better idea than the humanizing ethos of human rights to guide our praxis in today's world.

The recognition of human rights and the vindication of human dignity are increasingly universal phenomena. These rights are transcultural values proclaimed by all people of "good will". In today's world, religions are forced to accept these values if they want to be legitimized.

Only a religiosity that combines openness to the mystery of the sacred or divine with an effective passion for human beings and all that exists, as well as for a universal and fraternal vision of the human species, and that deeply assumes rationality, deserves to be called human. Humanism and religion belong together (MARDONES apud AMIGO FERNANDEZ DE ARROYABE 2003, p. 445-446).

From this point of view, human dignity should be the minimum requirement of every true religion.

In times of globalization, each religious tradition has been challenged to position itself in the debate with the others, which implies the need to think about the question of equality between all those who come together. This equality is facilitated by the recognition, by most religious traditions, of the golden rule that we should not do to others what we would not like them to do to us. On the other hand, the different texts, myths and rites make the question of equality difficult and some religions end up opting for a fundamentalist stance. In other words, while some religions open themselves up to dialogue, others close themselves off and set themselves up as absolute masters of the truth.

Equality and dialogue are fundamental elements in a democratic world. Such a position makes it necessary to profoundly re-evaluate the central traditions of all religions, starting from the principle that none of them is totally true or false. By forcing religious traditions to rethink their parameters, interreligious dialogue makes them open up to the world. Religions are not ends in themselves; they are, in fact, attempts to guide and give meaning to the lives of their followers through doctrines that claim to interpret the world.

These traditions are being forced by dialogue to be more modest in the face of the challenges that the contemporary world is posing.

Above doctrinal differences or religious practices, dialogue encourages theologians to assume the incomprehensible dimension of God and reality, and the faithful to develop an open solidarity by exchanging and reaffirming their own faith (BASSET 1999, p. 426).

This scenario transforms the absolute dimension of faith into the core of the meeting of believers in inter-religious dialogue, taking into account the truth that each believer brings. Dialogue opens up new perceptions of truth and the absolute in different religious traditions, and is therefore incompatible with any kind of fundamentalism that claims to possess absolute truths. On the level of doctrines, dialogue cannot go beyond the confrontations where each believer hides; on the level of faith, dialogue allows believers to meet in their deepest convictions, those that give meaning to their lives. Only faith, because it is a personal choice and not something that has been received to be passed on, can be revised and enriched through dialogue with other people who are guided along a different path.

3.3- Escaping fundamentalism: the articulation between ipse and idem identity

Faced with the depersonalization caused by globalization, the search for identity among the peoples who inhabit the planet is legitimate. One of the possible paths in this search can be guided by religious invariants that allow humanity to live a dignified way of life and to live in solidarity with different communities.

The different can be a threat to the established identity or it can help build a new identity without ceasing to be itself. In order to analyze this issue, Ricoeur (1991) distinguishes between two types of identity which end up being dialectically articulated. The idem identity is one that remains in time, it is fixed. Ipse identity, on the other hand, refers to identity as a process under construction. personal identity is constituted in a temporal dimension based on the diathesis of ipseity and sameness. We can't think of the idem of a person without the ipse and, in everyday life, they tend to overlap and confuse each other. In this process, character is formed, i.e. the set of marks that allows a person to be recognized.

The formation of the character that makes a person identifiable must, according to Ricoeur, be articulated with a second pole, ethics. In the ethics pole, the person guarantees the maintenance of themselves, which allows others to count on them. There is therefore an ethical dimension to ipseity, because someone counts on me and I am responsible for my actions towards the other. From the perspective of tradition versus construction, it is possible to reflect on inter-religious dialogue.

The process of internationalization requires the integration of globalization and universalization. This is a basic assumption. This integration involves articulating the ipse and idem identities of the cultures involved. Polarization in one of the identities can lead to fundamentalism (fixation on the idem identity) or loss of sameness (fixation on the ipse identity). The integration of these identities, on the other hand, keeps us as we are and leaves us open to the construction of the new.

Religions can facilitate or hinder this process. If they choose to articulate ipse and idem identities, they will affirm the need for dialogue. On the one hand, they will be defining their identity, and on the other, they will be opening up perspectives for learning from others and broadening their identity. The ethical principle that underpins character should guide the dialogue.

Ricoeur's analysis can be better explained by looking at the theological debate between the various religions. Christians, for example, have been forced to renounce their claim to be the masters of truth in the face of contemporary religious pluralism. Three basic lines of thought about the salvific legitimacy of each religion stand out among Christian theologians and prove this evolution from a fundamentalist to a pluralist stance (NOGUEIRA, 1997, p. 44-56):

- Exclusivism conditions salvation on the knowledge of a Jesus Christ who belongs to the church. The radical ecclesiocentrism of this current was overcome by the Council of Vatican II.

- Inclusivism affirms that salvation occurs in the various religions due to the mysterious presence of Jesus in them. The Christocentric cut here denies the salvific autonomy of the other religions by trying to imprint Christ's seal on them.

- Pluralism supports the salvific autonomy of each religion, removing the absolute character of Christianity in favor of the mystery of God as the ultimate reality. Christocentrism is replaced by theocentrism. Knitter (1986, p. 103), for example, proposes an approach of Christ together with religions and not against, above or in religions.

Some theologians still tend towards a dialectical view of these currents, moving towards open inclusivism. The transcendent presence of each religion is not excluded, but the incarnation is considered to be the highest point of the revelation of God's love for humanity, which makes a historical choice necessary. Panasiewicz (1997, p. 57-58) uses Ricoeur's (1991) terminology to analyze the open inclusivist proposal. Exclusivism and inclusivism would fixate on idem identity by defending Christian identity itself in the act of dialoguing. Relativism relates to ipse identity by focusing attention on becoming. Open inclusivism seeks the articulation of ipse-idem identities, because it punctuates identity and, at the same time, opens up perspectives for learning from the other. The open inclusivist position, as an intermediary position, would allow each religion to safeguard its identity and open itself up to learning from the others through dialogue.

3.4- Democracy and ethics

If we are really looking for a planetary ethic inspired by dialogue, we must admit that our culture is just one among others and give up any imperialist obsession. This implies taking on democracy as the only possible alternative for humanity. Democracy is not a perfect political regime, but it is the one that best serves the demands of human dignity. Throughout their history, national democratic projects have tried to reconcile political freedoms, social rights and a degree of social control over the economy. These projects have often failed due to the human inability to combine reason and tolerance in the pursuit of the common good. The challenge of humanity today is much more complex in that it goes beyond the boundaries of nation states. The success of a global democratic project depends on the human capacity to find minimum ethical references between different cultures (RIESGO 2003, p. 5). How do we find these references in a plural society?

Dialogue between different cultural and historical traditions must receive universal recognition. Human invariants must be found from this dialogue and then an ethics of minima will be built. This ethic of minima must be born out of an ethic of maxima. The latter refers to the demands of different human groups to live their diverse religious and moral experiences. The ethic of minima must arise from the dialogue between the ethic of maxima in order to make the democratic project possible. Interculturality is therefore an ally of democracy.

As early as the 15th century, the great discoveries brought awareness of a unified world. We live in a global village where people live together ever more closely. We share the same hopes and the needs of others are well known. Despite this, there is still a lack of solidarity, exploitation and wars. Thanks to planetary integration, however, it is no longer possible to run away from these problems and pretend they don't exist. Human consciousness has awakened to the need for pure fraternity, above private interests. In this context, religions have an important role to play: they must learn to look at differences while recognizing the divine origin of each one. Hegel had already stated that difference is what unites (LIMA VAZ 1999, p. 365).

Religious differences can inspire many conflicts but, on the other hand, they can also pacify them. Religions are, in themselves, ambivalent phenomena. They can arouse intense feelings and radical behavior. Nothing arouses both love and hate like religion. Conveniently matured, religion becomes a source of trust, openness and acceptance of others, of attitudes of understanding and forgiveness. On the other hand, failure to mature these early experiences can fulfill a regressive function that can lead to conflict and anguish. Religion then becomes a defense against lived reality, a protective shield against everyday anxiety. The ambivalence of religious experience lies precisely in the fact that it provides an opening to hope for life, while at the same time it can nourish despair. It can be a source of trust and a dangerous regression to childhood.

From another perspective, religious experience can be seen in terms of its positive potential for building a better world. The ёйес ideal is one of the major aspects of religious experience, alongside the trust generated by mystical experience. Every religious experience is linked to the desire for union between God and ethical demands. The ways in which the integration of the ethical dimensions is carried out, however, can also determine the destructive character of the religious experience for the human being himself. In other words, according to Morano (2002, p. 80), religious beliefs can become a factor of balance and personal and social development or, on the other hand, faith can become allied with destructive forces and increase conflicts. This is part of the essential ambiguity inherent in religious experience.

The ambiguous power of the religious element in different societies makes many fear it: on the one hand, it is capable of shaking up the established order by promoting revolution; on the other, it can numb the population and make them subservient to the powerful. Awareness of this ambivalence is fundamental if we are to look to the positive aspects of religions as a way of promoting intercultural dialogue and contributing to the construction of a new ethic for humanity. Peace today is only possible with a dialogue between civilizations that seeks a universal ethic. This ethic can and must be built through interreligious dialogue. It is not a code

objective; we are referring to a basic consensus on values and attitudes established by all religions and shared by believers.

The religions that are compatible with democracy and that can contribute to the realization of this project are humanizing religions: religions capable of overcoming the excesses of evasive spirituality and helping to form free subjects, endowed with conscience in the fight against suffering, injustice and oppression. They are religions that proclaim human dignity based on solidarity between peoples and human rights.

The religions to which this article refers - the "good" religions - are those that proclaim human dignity, personal autonomy and solidarity between peoples; humanizing religions. Cardinal Arns (2004, p. 341-352), noting the existence in the contemporary world of both authentic and distorted religions, affirms that true religions are geared towards peace, because they are born of the same supreme being. This being communicates with humanity in different ways, is present in all its relationships and encourages dialogue. Authentic religions awaken consciousness, making their followers critical of wars and fight for world peace. They encourage brotherly love and forgiveness, promoting communication between different cultures. False religions, on the other hand, numb the conscience. Only true religions, Cardinal Arns continues, offer proposals for ethical practice based on solidarity, which can be the source for establishing a minimum code of ethics for human coexistence. "In fact, the promotion of peace in the world is intrinsically ecumenical and interreligious" (ARNS 2004, p. 345).

An ethic built on inter-religious dialogue cannot accept exclusionary and intolerant religious projects, which are the hallmark of fundamentalist experiences. Much less "particular religions", typical of post-modernity, which examine the various strands of faith and choose the components that seem appropriate. It is true that many of today's religions trivialize God and end up becoming a product for immediate consumption. In these "religions", the faithful choose "a religion like they choose a brand of washing powder" (PRANDI apud WEISS, 2000, p. 86), or like they change the channel on the television. These post-modern "religions", which have sprung up in the supermarkets of faith, offer an evasive spirituality and lack content and depth.

3.5- Brazilian religious syncretism for the construction of a global ethic

Bearing in mind what has been said in the previous sections, this article defends the validity of Brazilian religious syncretism as a possible positive reference point for the issue of inter-religious dialogue. Syncretism is a practice of innovations and inventions of traditions. There is no universal character that establishes its limits or possibilities, which implies that its rational analysis can only be given on a case-by-case basis. Brazilian religious culture is made up of the articulation of various segments, both popular and erudite, which results in the establishment of all its diversity.

Unlike the post-modern religious supermarket, where people acquire teachings and rituals from different faiths to compose a personalized way of venerating the sacred, the religious syncretism of the Brazilian mystical fair is marked by the fusion of cults. Of course, Brazil has not been immune to the trade in the transcendent that is typical of post-modernity. Even this process, however, was done with the colors of the country: it was a trade without guilt, without fear of sangao, public and festive. Brazilian religious expressions have always been characterized by a lack of rigid contours, but unlike post-modern religions, which lack the break in level that characterizes true religions, they have managed to maintain their charm.

The harmony of this mystical fair serves to indicate ways of building a human project that overcomes the current fragmented rationality. In Brazil, religions have managed to harmonize efficiently. Each in its proper place, contributing cooperatively to collective behavior. In the chaos of desires, emotions and ideas that make up Brazilian society, Brazilian religious harmony - its efficient intuitive coordination - has managed to avoid, at least most of the time, the paths of fanaticism and excessive rationality, giving shape to our identity.

Cultural mixing has been the hallmark of Brazil since its discovery and the fundamental factor in its cultural identity. Cultures have interacted, coexisted and merged.

Historically, this process was not democratic and whites tried to eliminate black and indigenous culture. The cultural hybridity that resulted from this relationship was the way in which the dominated cultures survived. They made themselves present in the new culture through mestizaje.

The colonization of Brazil by Portugal was permeated by religious and mercantilist aspects. Colonization was, in itself, a hybrid between tradition and modernity, between rational action and religious belief. The metropole tried to impose its culture on the natives and Africans. The metropolitan project almost came to fruition, but the dominated cultures persisted. Through cultural mixing, they created an autonomous identity based on belief and emigration. This cultural identity emerged from the process of liberation from external impositions and the mutual influence of Western, indigenous and African culture. This spirit, the fruit of resistance to oppression, can constitute a path towards the integration of the human race in its search for profound truths and ways of life that bring individual and social happiness.

Brazil's spiritual identity has survived from the symbolic world of religious mestigagem. The path followed by the Brazilian people must be reflected upon for the present and the future. We are referring here to a historical, communitarian and symbolically integrated subject. This subject has shaped an ethical feeling based on religion. This experience of God leads to a horizontal dimension of coexistence between the members of society and a vertical dimension marked by mystery. The Brazilian symbolic world is marked by the integration of these dimensions, in which material elements take on transcendental dimensions. By understanding this religious experience, it is possible to go deeper into our identity and provide paths for humanity.

Brazilian religions have taken many paths in their history. A history that has always been marked by pluralism and syncretism, despite the predominance of Catholicism. Foreign cultural elements have been received, reinterpreted and mixed with local culture over the last 500 years, giving rise to new religious forms. Our history has been characterized by a plurality of voices that have blended together and this blending has become the main mechanism for social orientation in Brazil. Religious expressions, in particular, have brought an abundance of feelings, passions and sensuality, which makes it possible to talk about our syncretic structure with them.

The Brazilian Catholic religion has lived and continues to live surrounded by magical practices. Saints, Our Lady, sacraments, funeral rites, promises, pilgrimages to shrines, religious festivals and processions are part of everyday life and assure the faithful of earthly advantages. Christian practices are closely associated with indigenous, African and oriental traditions. At the same time as being Catholic, Brazilians attend spiritual sessions, commission "works", ask for protection from the Orishas and meditate in search of nirvana. All cultures coexist in a standardized way, despite their contradictions. Christian monotheism, indigenous animism and totemism and African fetishism coexist in harmony in the tropics, because "there is no sin below the equator".

Brazilians look to the sacred to manipulate the rules that govern the world through the magic of syncretism. The invocation of occult forces replaces rationality and gives meaning to our fragmented world. The people, deeply religious, live a religion without trauma, obsession with death or exaggerated passion. In the Pacs, there is a disconcerting intimacy with God, who is treated like a member of the family. This father God is neither punitive nor tragic, turning Brazilian religions into something sweet.

In short, each individual changes religions, syncretizes or belongs to more than one religious current, in a true insubordination to authority and institution. This exercise of Brazilian creativity, accentuated in times of globalization and democracy, originated in the colonial past and has forced religious institutions to adapt, throughout history, to the Brazilian way of being.

In the process of adapting these religious manifestations, there are elements of homogenization originating in the clash of matrices that populates the Brazilian universe of the sacred and defines models of conduct. The melting pot mixes and processes differences, allowing the intercommunication of symbolic universes through syncretism and the relativization of institutional dogmas, which are replaced by dialogues. Despite the existence of modernizing outbreaks advocating the purification of syncretistic tendencies, they are too deeply rooted, and such outbreaks end up succumbing to the porosity of Brazilian religiosity. Modernizing discourses have never prevented the Brazilian people from continuing to adopt their characteristic hybrid conduct, which increasingly brings religious diversity and complexity. And it is precisely this overlap that can inspire the world on the path to peace.

Mestizaje in Brazil has become an agent of civilization. We are a hybrid country, which gives us our identity and can be our specific contribution to the world. We have learned to merge codes in a joyful and festive way, which has generated a deep fraternization of values and feelings from the religious cultures that have made up the country. A mixture of codes and people that created a world conducive to generalized exchange. The carnivalization of life favors dialogue, since it makes us open to agreements and conciliation. Brazil is far from the utopia proposed by intercultural philosophy, but the dream of a harmonious world seems to be producing some concrete results in this country. Even if only hints of a better world are found here, they can serve as hope for those who dream of a world based on intercultural respect.

Accepting the contribution of the Brazilian mystical fair means, in practice, a radical self-criticism of philosophy, a de-philosophizing, which frees philosophy from the hegemony of the Western European tradition and from academic institutionalization according to the canon of that tradition. It means breaking away from the reigning monoculturalism in philosophy, taking the opposite path to Heidegger, who had an "esoteric conception of philosophy", claiming its extemporaneous character (FORNET-BETANCOURT, 2001, p. 296). This thesis accepts contextual philosophies and allows itself to be seduced by the various cultural traditions, their symbolic universes, their imaginaries, their memories and rites. They would not be objects of study, but the living words of subjects who can learn and teach together.

4. Islamic fundamentalism

4.1- Historical origins of Islamic fundamentalism

The history of the relationship between the West and Islam has been in increasing crisis over the last few decades. Proof of this is the increase in the number of terrorist attacks of a religious-Islamic nature after September 11, 2001. Sklarz (2006) defends the idea that many generalizations have been made to explain this conflict. Claiming that the root of this crisis lies in social inequality, the violence of fanatical Islamists or a supposed oppression imposed by the West on Muslims for centuries means treating the issue in a dangerously superficial way. Such statements treat Islam as a monolithic bloc, which is a falsehood: just as the West brings together the most diverse ethnicities, Islam includes people of the most varied tendencies and a tradition of enormous diversity.

Sklarz (2006) also states that experts believe that suicide attacks are not driven by madness or poverty, but by facts and ideas that have a history and have marked the trajectory of Islam. This idea is defended by the main leader of Islamic fundamentalism today, Saudi Osama Bin Laden. In a video from October 7, 2001, posted on the Internet after the attacks on the twin towers in the United States, he spoke of the humiliation that Islam has suffered for more than eighty years. It is these eighty years to which he refers that explain the current crisis between the West and Islam.

Between the decline of the Roman Empire and the advent of modernity, Islam remained at the forefront of the human development process. This leadership began in the seventh century of the Christian era, when the followers of the Prophet Muhammad set out from Medina, in present-day Saudi Arabia, and conquered the Middle East, North Africa and the Ulster Peninsula. The Catholic Church's attempts to recover the Holy Land through the crusades in the 11th century met with resounding failure.

According to British historian Bernard Lewis, Dean of Princeton University, "Islam was the greatest military power on earth. Its armies were invading Europe, Africa, India and China at the same time" (LEWIS, apud SKLARZ, 2006, p. 66). It was 1ашЬёш the main economic and commercial power. "In the arts and sciences, it had reached a level never before attained in history" (LEWIS, apud SKLARZ, 2006, p. 66).

From the 16th century onwards, however, Europeans promoted the Renaissance in the arts and caught up in science. The forefront of history left the realm of Islam and passed into the hands of Christianity. Spain, Portugal, Austria and Russia won successive military battles against the Alawite ex-drites. By the end of the 17th century, when the Ottoman Turks were its main political representatives, Islam was already a decadent force. The West, for its part, had renewed its values with the French Revolution and the Industrial Revolution. After World War I, the Ottoman Empire finally collapsed. Its spoils were divided between the French and the British, who parcelled out the lands of the Middle East, inventing a division into three entities with new borders and names. Two of them, Iraq and Palestine (today Jordan, the West Bank and Israel), remained under British mandate. The French controlled the third, called Syria (today Syria and Lebanon). It is to this moment that Bin Laden refers when he speaks of the eighty years of humiliation of Islam. World War I turned the Muslim world into a colony of European empires.

After World War II and decolonization, many Arab governments followed the path of modernity and restricted the influence of Islamic law. They then began to import ideologies such as socialism and nationalism. The Egyptian dictator Gamal Abdel Nasser and the Libyan dictator Muamar Gaddafi stood out in this process, preaching the unity of all Arabs under the banner of pan-Arabism. The initiative did not work. The defeat by the Israelis discredited Arab nationalism. The result of this new frustration was the opening up of the Islamic world to a revolutionary ideology.

This new ideology started from the premise that Islam had taken the wrong path, because its rulers had adopted the laws and customs of the infidels. It was necessary to establish regimes that followed an extreme interpretation of the Sharia, Islamic law. One of the movements behind this idea was Salafism (from salaf al-salih, or "the venerable ancestors"), which calls for a return to the purity of Muhammad's time, if necessary through violence. In 1928, Salafism gave rise in Egypt to the Muslim Brotherhood, the mother of almost all current Muslim fundamentalist groups, such as Hamas, Al Qaeda and Islamic Jihad. The Brotherhood's motto was: "God is our goal; the Koran is our constitution; the Prophet is our leader; struggle is our path; and death in the name of God is our greatest aspiration" (SKLARZ, 2006, p. 68).

Islamists are divided into various currents, but it is no exaggeration to say that they have reinvented religion. The first innovation was to reformulate the concept of jihad, now known as "holy war", but whose original meaning is "struggle or striving to live according to divine law". This new concept of jihad, often manifested through terrorist acts, transformed what had previously been national conflicts into religious ones.

Samuel Huntington (1997) analyzed this paradigm shift in the Arab world, saying that the world was entering a new phase in which conflicts would have their origins in cultural aspects. He argues that the biggest difference and source of war is between the West and Islam. This theory generated a great deal of controversy because it implied the idea of an "Islamic threat" and denied the possibility that the West and Islam could live together in harmony. Huntington's theses were considered prejudiced against Islamists.

Certainly, to say that there is a clash between the West and Islam is to simplify history too much. What is more likely is that there are several clashes in progress. The most notable of these is between European Muslim immigrants and the countries that have received them. There is a feeling among these Muslim immigrants and their children that they are not part of the country that welcomed them. They find themselves in an identity dilemma that deepens their sense of frustration or hatred. "They end up being easy prey for radical Islam, because they seek in it their lost identity" (ARISTEGUI, apud SKLARZ, 2006, p. 69).

Another striking clash on the old continent is between Islam and European xenophobia. In Denmark, where the newspaper Jyllands Posten published the famous cartoons of Mohammed, there is a growing flirtation between voters and ultra-right-wing candidates who believe that Denmark would be a better country if only white-skinned Christians lived there. And France's interior minister, Nicolas Sarkozy, called the young Muslims responsible for the disturbances in the Paris suburbs "scum".

A third clash would be within Islam itself, between radicals and moderates, between those who defend states based on the law of the Koran and those who want nations with separation between religion and the state. For many, stimulating this rift is the only effective way to combat fundamentalism.

The last clash would involve the West and the major religions, including Islam. The clash we are seeing is perhaps only part of a much wider one. Western values, such as democracy, individualism and human rights, are not in line with the values of the great religions. The latter consider that the only source of legitimacy is God and the West, especially since the French Revolution, has managed to separate - at least formally - religion from politics.

In this context, apart from the conflicts that routinely occur in Iraq and Afghanistan, Sklarz (2006) highlights the following as hotspots of religious tension involving Islam in recent years: Sudan, Georgia, Kosovo, Kashmir, Chechnya, the Philippines, Palestine and Xingjiang.

4.2- The question of fundamentalism and its main Islamic representative at the beginning of the 21st century: Al Qaeda

Fundamentalism was born in the South of the United States at the beginning of the 20th century as a reaction against "modernism" in theology, against literary criticism of biblical texts, against scientific research. Its main criticism was against the Darwinism that was spreading through society. In opposition to the Darwinist theory of the evolution of species, fundamentalists sought to reaffirm the biblical account of creation.

Regardless of whether we're talking about Catholic, Protestant or Islamic fundamentalism, the central point of these religious currents is to cling to the written word in its literal sense. Fundamentalism is based on the idea that the sacred text was revealed by God and this position avoids any kind of controversy. In fact, it is precisely because they have a single God that believers in monotheistic religions conclude that their truth is unique and are more likely to become fundamentalists.

In the case of the Koran specifically, rather than being revealed, the Holy Book was "generated" directly by God. The fact that Allah himself "generated" the Law makes Muslims, more than any believers of any other religion, potential fundamentalists. Such a monotheistic conception radically rejects the secular state and a Law not revealed by God.

The problem of Islamic fundamentalism is directly linked to the context of the Cold War. The key point here was the great game of political interests at the time, often to the detriment of collective interests and respect for nations. The alliances formed during the Cold War were based on geopolitical interests, leaving ideological and cultural differences aside. Coups d'état, military dictatorships and radical Islamist groups were fomented in order to expand the superpowers' zones of influence.

When referring to terrorism in the current Muslim context, Wellausen (2002) considers three major groups as categories of terrorist organizations. These are: 1) Groups partially controlled by a state; 2) Terrorists with well-defined issues and local agendas; 3) Pan-Islamic terrorist groups that wage global war against "the enemies of Islam", such as the pan-Islamic group Al Qaeda, which was responsible for the attacks on the US, directed at the World Trade Center and the Pentagon, on September 11, 2001.

Al-Qaeda became notorious at the end of the 20th century and the beginning of the 21st for its extremely violent actions and the media spotlight it received. Al-Qaeda had a highly sophisticated communications structure that involved TV channels and websites. Often using homemade recordings of acts or threats of terror, it was able to generate fear and panic among the world's population. These recordings were always followed by prayers and seen by their followers as great achievements in the history of Islam. The organization argued that Western governments, and particularly the US government, were acting against the interests of Muslims.

In addition to the attacks of September 11, 2001, Al-Qaeda is believed to have been involved in the following attacks, among others:

- American Embassy in Nairobi, Kenya, on August 7, 1998;
- American Embassy in Dar es Salaam, Tanzania, on August 7, 1998;
- USS Cole bomber, attacked in Lemen, October 12, 2000;
- Attacks on the London Underground on July 7, 2005.

As stated earlier, Al Qaeda originated in the context of the Cold War and was a by-product of the US government's alliance policy. In order to contain the growing Soviet expansion towards Central Asia and the Gulf, the US began to finance arms for the

Afghan guerrillas. A kind of pact was then established between the Islamist *jihadists* and the US government. However, in order to appear "invisible" in this context, the US government used supposed humanitarian agencies in Pakistan to fund Afghan fighters *(mujahidin).*

The fight that the Afghan Muslims waged against the USSR was not merely a religious and ideological issue. The atheism and communism propagated by the Soviets was a secondary issue to the territorial and power dispute: the sovereignty of Afghanistan was at stake. In this process, the United States financed the Islamic radicals with the aim of weakening the Soviets. The US government was never interested in promoting human rights or democracy. Given this, it is not surprising that there is an Afghan revolt against the US, which has used the Islamic world as a puppet for its own interests.

4.3- Terrorist Osama Bin Laden

The collective imagination, when referring to Al Qaeda, makes a direct association between this movement and its leader, Osama Bin Laden. With reference to the Weberian analysis of power, we can classify his leadership as charismatic. In other words, it is expressed "in the extracotid veneration of the sanctity, heroic power or exemplary character of a person and the orders revealed or created by them" (Weber, 2004, p. 141). Charisma should be understood as an extraordinary quality that a person possesses (real, pretended or presumed). What matters, and this stands out in Osama Bin Laden's leadership, is his followers' hero worship.

It is in the Afghan War that we find the origin of the hero myth created around this leader. It seems that there is an inseparable historical link in this issue, which allows us to say that the hard core of Al Qaeda comes directly from this war. On the other hand, it is also possible to link this organization to an older one, the Society of Muslim Brothers, founded in 1928 by Sayyd Qutb. The influence ideology and action strategies of this group was passed on to Al Qaeda. The Muslim Brotherhood's aim was to form an Islamic state in Egypt, expel Western militias and companies and restore the tenets of Islam to the daily life of Egyptian society. It represents the foundations of contemporary Islamic fundamentalism.

Al Qaeda is fighting to unify the Muslim world around a single cause, to expel the foreign exdrites from the Muslim territory occupied during the First Gulf War in 1991.

The war against the West is, from this perspective, a war for the autonomy and sovereignty of the Arab Islamic world (SUGAHARA, 2008, p. 55).

The charisma of the Saudi is evident when we remember the American failure to capture Bin Laden despite the million-dollar efforts of the US government after the September 11 attack. In this process of forming the charisma of the terrorist leader, there is a paradoxical component in that the United States, in its eagerness to weaken the former USSR, was responsible for creating the image of the war hero and charismatic leader.

One point deserves to be highlighted in the perspective defended by Osama Bin Laden: he has succeeded, at least in the Islamic world, in creating the image of a violent West that violates the Muslim East. Using the expression "International Front for Jihad against the Jews and Crusaders" to designate the movement he leads, Osama has consolidated his image to the detriment of the American image. According to Samuel Huntington (1997), the West has succeeded in conquering the world through organized violence, and not through its superiority in ideas, values or religion. Recent international terrorism would be the counterpoint to this Western violence. In other words, the more American troops commit abuses in Iraq or Afghanistan, the more Bin Laden's charisma is consolidated.

Osama Bin Laden was born in 1957 to Mohammed Bin Laden, one of the richest men in Saudi Arabia. He came into contact with religious circles from an early age. In 1980, when Soviet troops invaded Afghanistan, he was 23 years old. He was chosen to lead the war against the Soviets by the Americans a year later. With funds from his family and the CIA, he sent engineers to Pakistan and Afghanistan to build tunnels, roads and ammunition dumps in the mountains.

Bin Laden proclaimed himself leader of the war against the USSR and created his own battle line in 1986. Volunteers from all over the world arrived in Afghanistan to serve him. He transformed his fighting network into an international terrorist structure, with the aim of establishing a state within the secular state. In 1988, the Al Qaeda group was created to control the entry and exit of people through Pakistan and Afghanistan, serving as a support for the recruitment of soldiers in the different Arab countries. Al Qaeda began to form alliances with other terrorist groups such as AL - Jihad and Hezbollah, with the aim of forming a united group in the face of the common enemy which, after the

Soviet defeat, was already the West and, above all, the United States. Bin Laden also created networks with the Armed Islamic Groups of Algeria, the Philippines, the Middle East, North Africa and New York. Terrorism, in Bin Laden's view, is the best way to respond to the injustices practiced against minorities by expressing a struggle on a global scale.

5. Final thoughts

The issue of terrorism, especially that linked to Islamic fundamentalism, can be analyzed bearing in mind the concept of risk society developed by Ulrich Beck and Anthony Giddens (1997). The authors state that the risk society is a stage in which the threats produced begin to take shape, i.e. a phase in which social, political, economic and individual risks escape institutional controls. In other words, a risk society is one that is about to break with its past, shaking up the dominant social structure. In this type of society, unpredictability and insecurity become constant in the lives of individuals. Terror, which threatens individuals with violent death, breaks the balance once established by the state and disrupts the social web that guarantees cultural and political development.

According to Beck and Giddens, fundamentalist terrorism represents a crisis of traditional local power in the face of the expansion of globalization. "*The construction of Islamic identity takes place as a reaction against unattainable modernization (capitalist or socialist), the negative effects of globalization and the collapse of the post-colonial nationalist project*" (CASTELLS, 2002:35).

The major problem posed by the risk society is the distorted perception that individuals come to have of reality. Risk makes people see the world as a risk instead of identifying the risks in the world. This in itself causes the individual to become incapable of acting, which is one of the two pitfalls caused by terrorism. The other pitfall is the loss of individual freedom. Unable to act, people give up their individual freedom in the name of supposed security, making them an easy target for government manipulation. The result of this process is the paralysis of society.

Sugahara (2008), Habermas (2001), Giddens (2005), Bauman (1998) and Beck (1997) all share the same rationale when addressing the dilemma between freedom and security. Terrorist groups have managed to co-opt more and more individuals who are unhappy with the direction of modernity. On the other hand, many states use the fear and insecurity in society to wage war against terrorism, suppressing freedom and individual rights.

Terrorism shakes up structures and subverts society's perception of globalization. Concepts such as security, democracy and freedom are constantly being altered. For the sake of security, people tend to give up the two basic pillars of modernity, freedom and democracy. As Sugahara (2008: VI) summarizes, *"the widespread threat of international terrorism is perceived as a form of contemporary malaise that usurps individual freedom in the name of collective security".* We are therefore dealing with two different issues: the question of terrorism itself and the question of the authoritarian reaction of national states to this threat.

According to Ramoneda (2000: 22-23), we are experiencing a paradox: fear of the other favors national cohesion around power and makes citizens less demanding of those who govern, who are also those who protect them. Social cohesion through fear is maintained because it is necessary to defend oneself against the so-called "barbarians". After September 11, 2001, Islam and barbarism were identified and satanized. What is forgotten in this unquestionable image is that the reaction of states to terrorism is also a form of barbarism.

This research highlights Benjamin's statement (1985: 225): "there has never been a monument of culture that was not also a monument of barbarism. And just as culture is not free of barbarism, neither is the process of transmitting culture". The barbaric is not external, but internal to the movement of the creation and transmission of culture, it is what causes horror in those who contemplate the triumphal procession of the victors trampling the bodies of the vanquished and know the nail of infamy in every monument of civilization. There is no doubt that the terrorist attacks perpetrated by Islamic fundamentalists are barbaric. On the other hand, the violent reactions of "democratic" states and the passive abdication of the citizens of these states, for the sake of security, of values such as freedom and democracy, are no less barbaric.

Modernity has witnessed a double movement that could be fatal. On the one hand, it has displaced religion from the public to the private sphere. Religion has been treated as an archaism that would be overcome by the march of reason or science, thus disregarding the needs it responds to and the symbolisms it involves. On the other hand, we are witnessing the shrinking of the state in the area of social rights. Spiritual emptiness goes hand in hand with economic and social exclusion, poverty and unemployment. The articulation between secularization, the neoliberal state and the postmodern condition of insecurity generated by the fear of the ephemeral, leads us to understand two facets of contemporary barbarism: religious fundamentalism and the widespread acceptance of violent reaction by states.

The return of religious fundamentalism presents us with a risk of immense proportions. Firstly, because modernity has driven religion into the private sphere, and today the shrinking of the public sphere and the shrinking of the private sphere could once again give religions the role of social order and cohesion. Secondly, because history has already shown the effects of this order and cohesion promoted by religion.

Spinoza's (1988) criticism of religious theological power is highly suggestive of this risk: he states that men, desirous and insecure, experience fear and hope. Their fear gives rise to superstition and religion. People ignore the real causes of events and things, because they ignore the necessary order and connection of all things and the real causes of their feelings and agonies, they imagine that everything depends on some omnipotent will that creates and governs all things according to designs unreachable by human reason. This is why they abdicate reason as a capacity for knowing reality and expect religion not only to explain it, but also to dispel fear and increase hope. Now, says Spinoza, there is no more effective means of dominating men than keeping them in fear and hope, but there is also no more effective means of making them seditious and fickle than changing the causes of fear and hope.

Spinoza's criticism of religious power can also be applied to unchecked state power. Just like religions, states are capable of fixing the forms and contents of superstition. While it is necessary to understand and criticize fundamentalism, it is also necessary to understand and criticize the reaction of states to terrorism. The democratic project requires examining and demolishing both the foundations of theological-political power and of states.

Theological-political power and the power of the state granted by frightened individuals is doubly violent: firstly, because it aims to rob men of the origin of their social and political actions; secondly, because they prevent the exercise of freedom, since they not only regulate habits and customs, but also language and thought, seeking to dominate not only bodies, but also spirits. Powerful states and fundamentalist groups aim to ensure obedience and voluntary servitude, making men consider it honorable to shed their blood and that of others to satisfy the ambition of a few.

References

ARNS, Paulo Evaristo. "Peace and Religions": *Revista Estudos Avangados I* Universidade de Sao Paulo, n. 52, p. 341-352, 2004.

ARISTEGUI, Gustavo. *Islam against Islam.* Barcelona: Ediciones B, 2004.

ARROYABE, Maria Luisa Amigo Fernandez. 2003. *Humanism for the 21st Century.* Bilbao: University of Deusto.

BARRETO, Maria Amalia Pereira. Syncretism. In: SILVA, Benedito (dir). *Dicionario de Ciencias Sociais.* Rio de Janeiro: Getulio Vargas Foundation, 1986.

BASSET, Jean-Claude. *Interreligious Dialogue: Opportunity for Faith or Decline of the Same.* Bilbao: Desclde de Brouwer, 1999.

BASTIDE, Roger. *Brazil.* Land of stories. Paris: Hachette, 1957.

. "Contribution to the study of Catholic-Fetishist syncretism". In: BASTIDE, Roger (dir.). *Estudos Afro-Brasileiros, Perspectiva.* Sao Paulo: s/e, p. 159-191, 1973.

. *Le Sacre Sauvage et autres essais.* Paris: Payot, 1975.

BAUMAN, Zygmunt. *The Malaise of Post-Modernity.* Rio de Janeiro: Jorge Zahar Editora, 1998.

BENJAMIN, Walter. "The concept of history". Selected works. *Magic and technique.* Art and Politics. Sao Paulo: Brasiliense, 1985.

BECK, Ulrich & GIDDENS, Anthony & LASH, Scott. *Reflexive Modernization.* Sao Paulo: Editora da Universidade Estadual Paulista, 1997.

CASTELLS, Manuel. *The Power of Identity.* Sao Paulo: Paz e Terra, 2002.

CHAMPION, Frangoise. Fluctuating religiosity, eclecticism and syncretism. In: DELUMEAU, Jean (dir.). *The great religions of the world.* Lisbon: Proenga publishing house, 1996.

CHAUI, Marilena. "Religious fundamentalism: the question of theological-political power". In: BORON, Atilo. *Contemporary Political Philosophy: Controversies on Civilization, Empire and Citizenship.* Sao Paulo: Department of Political Science. Faculty of Philosophy, Letters and Human Sciences. University of Sao Paulo, April 2006.

DINIZ, Eugenio. "Understanding the Phenomenon of Terrorism: New Challenges for Peacebuilding". In: *Peace and Terrorism.* Sao Paulo: Editora Hucitec, 2004.

DURKHEIM, Emile. *Suicide.* Sao Paulo: Martins Fontes, 2000.

ESPINOSA, Baruch. *Theological-Political Treatise.* Lisbon: Imprensa Nacional/Casa da Moeda, 1988.

FERNANDES, Goncalves. *Religious Syncretism in Brazil.* Curitiba: Guaira, 1941.

FERRETI, Sergio F. "Notas sobre o sincretismo religioso no Brasil - modelos, limitagoes, possibilidades". *Revista Tempo,* n. 11, p. 13-26, 2001.

. *Rethinking Syncretism.* Sao Paulo: EDUSP-FAPEMA, 1995.

. Afro-Brazilian Syncretism and Cultural Resistance. In: CAROSO, Carlos; BACELAR, Jeferson (dir.). *Faces of Afro-Brazilian Tradition.* Rio de Janeiro: Pallas, 113-130, 1999.

FORNET-BETANCOURT, Raul. Filosofia e interculturalidad en América Latina: intento de introduction no filosofica, In: ARNAIZ, Graciano Gonzalez R. (org.) *El discurso intercultural:* Prolegomenos a una filosofia intercultural. Madrid, Biblioteca Nueva, p. 107-120, 2002.

. *Intercultural transformation of philosophy.* Bilbao: Desclee, 2001.

FREUD, S. (1939). *L'homme Moise et la religion monoteiste.* Paris: Gallimard, 1986.

. (1915) "Considbrations actuelles sur la guerre et sur la mort". In: *Essais de Psychanalyse.* Paris: Payot, p. 7-115, 1984.

. (1933) "Pourquoi la guerre?" In: *Resultats, idees, problemes II.* Paris: PUF, p. 203-215, 1992.

GIDDENS, Anthony. *World Out of Control.* Rio de Janeiro: Record publishing house, 2005.

HABERMAS, Jurgen. *The Post-National Constellation.* Sao Paulo: Littera Mundi, 2001.

HUNTINGTON, Samuel P. *The Clash of Civilizations.* Rio de Janeiro: Editora Objetiva, 1997.

KIENZLER, Klaus. *Religious fundamentalism.* Madrid: Alianza, 2000.

KNITTER, Paul. "Catholic theology of religions at a crossroads". *Concilium Magazine,* n. 202, p. 103-113, 1986.

LEWIS, Bernard. *What Went Wrong in the Middle East?* Rio de Janeiro: Jorge Zahar, 2002.

MARX, Karl. *Manuscripts:* Economics and Philosophy. Madrid: Alianza, 1986.

MIJOLLA-MELLO, Sophie. *The need to know.* Paris: Dunod, 2002.

. "Terrorism, Barbarism and Disorder. Part IF'. *Psiquiatria Clinica,* v. 2, n. 17, p. 173-183, 2005.

. *Leplaisir depensee.* Paris: PUF, 1992.

NOVAES, Regina. "Young people without religion: secularizing winds, 'spirit of the times' and new syncretisms". *RevistaEstudos Avangados,* Sao Paulo, n. 52, p. 321-330, 2004.

MORANO, Carlos Dominguez. "Ambivalence of religion". *Revista Frontera,* n. 23, p. 29-80, 2002.

NOGUEIRA, Luiz Eustaquio dos Santos. "The Christian challenged by religions". *Horizonte - revista do nucleo de estudos de teologia,* n. 2, p. 44-56, 1997.

PANASIEWICZ, Roberlei. "Internationalization, identity, and interreligious dialogue". *Horizonte - revista do nucleo de estudos de teologia,* n. 2, p. 57-61, 1997.

PAPE, Robert. "The Strategic Logic of Suicide Terrorism". *American Political Science Review,* v. 93, n. 3, p. 4, 2003.

PROCOPIO, Argemiro. "Terrorism and international relations". *Revista Brasileira de Politica Internacional,* v.. 2, n. 44, p. 62-81, 2001.

RAMONEDA, Josep. *After the political box.* Sao Paulo: Editora SENAC, 2000.

RICOEUR, Paul. *Le conflit des interpretations.* Essais d'hermeneutique. Paris: Seuil, 1969.

. *Hermeneuticaypsicoanalisis.* Buenos Aires: Aurora, 1975.

RICOEUR, Paul. *The self as other.* Campinas: Papirus, 1991.

RIESGO, Manuel Fernandez del. *The social ambiguity of religion.* Navarra: Editorial Verbo Divino, 1997.

. *The enigma of the human condition: a dialog between reason and faith.* La Ciudad de Dios: Real Monasterio de el escorial, 2002.

. *Faith and human dignity:* A religion for democracy (Unpublished).

. "Globalization, interculturality, religion and democracy". *Revista ciencias de las religiones,* n. 8, p. 5-28, 2003.

ROUANET, Sergio Paulo. "Latin America between globalization and universalization": *Revista Tempo Brasileiro*, n. 122, p. 59-72, 1995.

. "Faith and suspicion in Freud". *Folha de Sao Paulo,* Caderno Mais, p. 6, October 30, 2005.

SANCHIS, Pierre. "P'ra não dizer que não falei de Sincretismo". *ISER Communications,* n. 45, p. 4-11, 1994.

. "The religions of Brazilians". *Horizonte: revista do nucleo de estudos de teologia,* n. 2, p. 28-43, 1997.

SKLARZ, Eduardo. "War of the worlds". *Superinteressante,* n. 229, p. 66-71, 2006.

SUGAHARA, Thiago Yoshiaki Lopes. *Terrorism and insecurity in the post-9/11 world.* Master's dissertation in International Relations, UNESP, Sao Paulo, 2008.

VALENTE, Waldemar. *Sincretismo Religioso Afro-Brasileiro*, Sao Paulo: Nacional, 1976.

VAZ, Henrique Claudio Lima. *Writings on Philosophy IV:* Introduction to philosophical ethics 1. Sao Paulo: Loyola, 1999.

VATTIMO, Gianni. *Etica de la interpretation.* Barcelona: Piados, 1991.

WEISS, Bruno. "The good and the banal": *RevistaIstoE*, n. 1579, p. 85-86, 2000.

WELLAUSEN, Saly da Silva. "Terrorism and the September 11 attacks". *Tempo sociologico,* v.14, n.2, p.83-112, 2002.

Printed by Books on Demand GmbH, Norderstedt / Germany